ST. JOHN PASSION

in Full Score

Johann Sebastian Bach

From the Bach-Gesellschaft Edition
Edited by Wilhelm Rust

DOVER PUBLICATIONS, INC.
New York

Published in Canada by General Publishing Company, Ltd., 30 Lesmill Road, Don Mills, Toronto, Ontario.

Bibliographical Note

This Dover edition, first published in 1993, is an unabridged republication of *Passions-musik nach dem Evangelisten Johannes*, which forms part of Vol. 12 of *Johann Sebastian Bach's Werke, herausgegeben von der Bach-Gesellschaft zu Leipzig*, edited by Wilhelm Rust and published by Breitkopf & Härtel, Leipzig, 1863. The editor's foreword has been omitted, and lists of voices and instruments have been added.

Library of Congress Cataloging-in-Publication Data

Bach, Johann Sebastian, 1685–1750.
   [Johannespassion]
   St. John Passion : in full score / Johann Sebastian Bach ; from the Bach-Gesellschaft edition edited by Wilhelm Rust.
   1 score.
   Reprint. Originally published: Passionsmusik nach dem Evangelisten Johannes. Leipzig : Breitkopf & Härtel, 1863. (Bach's Werke ; Jahrg. 12, 1).
   ISBN 0-486-27755-0
   1. Oratorios—Scores. 2. Passion music. I. Rust, Wilhelm, 1822–1892. II. Title.
M2000.B15J64   1993   93-36940
                                                            CIP
                                                             M

Manufactured in the United States of America
Dover Publications, Inc., 31 East 2nd Street, Mineola, N.Y. 11501

ST. JOHN PASSION

Words by B. H. Brockes and others, arranged by Bach
Music by Johann Sebastian Bach

VOICES AND CHARACTERS

Evangelist	Tenor
Jesus	Bass
Petrus [Peter]	Bass
Magd [Maid]	Soprano
Diener [Servant]	Tenor

Soprano, Alto, Tenor and Bass Soli

Chorus [SATB]   (*Coro*)

INSTRUMENTATION

2 Flutes (*Flauto traverso I & II*)

2 Oboes (*Oboe I & II*)

Oboe d'Amore

2 Oboes da Caccia (*Oboe da caccia I & II*)

Violin I (*Violino I*)

Violin II (*Violino II*)

Viola

2 Violas d'Amore (*Viola d'amore I & II*)

Viola da Gamba

Lute (*Liuto*)

Organ and Continuo (*Organo e Continuo*)

(Continuo: Cellos, Bassoons, Double Bass) (*Violoncelli, Bassoni, Violone*)

CONTENTS

Erster Theil. (First Part)

Zweiter Theil. (Second Part)

Anhang. (Supplement).

FIRST PART

CORO.

10

Da Capo.

RECITATIVO.

Evangelist.

Evangelist.
Jesus.

Je_sus ging mit sei_nen Jüngern ü_ber den Bach Kidron, da war ein Garten, darein ging Je_sus und seine Jünger. Judas a_ber, der ihn ver_rieth, wusste den Ort auch, denn Jesus versammle_te sich oft daselbst mit sei_nen Jüngern. Da nun Ju_das zu sich hat_te ge_nommen die Schaar, und der Ho_hen_priester und Pha_ri_sä_er Diener, kommt er da_hin mit Fackeln, Lampen und mit Waffen. Als nun Je_sus wusste Al_les, was ihm be_gegnen soll_te, ging er hin _aus, und sprach zu ih_nen: Wen su_chet ihr? Sie antwor_te_ten ihm:

CORO.

Oboe I.
Oboe II.
Flauto traverso I. II,
Violino I.
Violino II.
Viola.

Soprano. — Jesum, Jesum, Jesum von Nazareth, Jesum von Nazareth, Je_sum von Na_zareth!

Alto. — Jesum, Jesum, Jesum von Nazareth, Jesum von Nazareth, Jesum von Na_zareth!

Tenore. — Jesum, Jesum, Jesum von Nazareth, Jesum von Nazareth, Jesum von Na_zareth!

Basso. — Jesum, Jesum, Jesum von Nazareth, Jesum von Nazareth, Jesum von Na_zareth!

Organo e Continuo.

17

18

RECITATIVO.

Evangelist.

Evangelist.

Die Schaar a_ber und der O_ber_hauptmann, und die Diener der Ju_den nahmen Je_sum und bun_den ihn, und füh_reten ihn auf's er_ste zu Hannas, der war Ca_iphas Schwäher, welcher des Jah_res Ho_her_priester war. Es war aber Ca_iphas, der den Juden rieth, es wäre gut, dass ein Mensch würde um_bracht für das Volk.

Organo e Continuo.

ARIA.

Oboe I.

Oboe II.

Alto.

Organo e Continuo.

piano

piano

Von den Stri _ _ _ _ cken-mei _ ner

piano

Sün _ _ den _ mich zu entbin _ den, mich zu entbin _ _ den, wird mein Heil ge _ bun _ _ _ den;

von den Stri _ cken

mei _ ner Sün _ _ _ _ den mich zu ent _ bin _ den, mich zu ent _ bin _ _ den, wird mein Heil ge _ bun _

den; von den Stricken mei _ _ ner Sün _ den mich zu ent _ bin _ den,

mich zu ent_bin_den, mich zu ent_bin_den, wird mein Heil_ge_bun_den.

Mich von al_len La_ster_beu_len völ_lig zu hei_

len, völlig zu hei_len, mich von al_len

RECITATIVO.

Evangelist.

Si_mon Pe_trus a_ber fol_ge_te Je_su nach, und ein an_d'rer Jün_ger.

Organo e Continuo.

RECITATIVO.

**Evangelist. Jesus.
Petrus. Magd. Diener.**

Organo e Continuo.

Dersel_bige Jünger war dem Hohenpriester bekannt, und ging mit Je_su hinein in des Hohenpriesters Pallast. Petrus a_ber stund draussen vor der Thür. Da ging der andere Jünger, der dem Hohenpriester be_kannt war, hin_aus, und re_dete mit der Thür_hüte_rin und füh_rete Pe_trum hinein. Da sprach die Magd, die Thür_hüte_rin, zu Pe_tro: Bist du nicht dieses Menschen Jünger ei_ner? Er sprach: Ich bin's nicht! Es stunden a_ber die Knechte und Diener, und hatten ein Kohlfeu'r gemacht, (denn es war kalt,) und wär_ _meten sich. Pe_trus a_ber stund bei ih_nen, und wär_me_te sich. A_ber der Ho_he_prie_ster frag_te Je_sum um sei_ne Jünger und um sei_ne Leh_re. Je_sus antwor_te_te ihm: Ich ha_be frei,

32

33

ARIA.
Tutti li Stromenti.

38

Her_zen stehn die Schmerzen mei_ner Mis _ _ se _ that, mei _ _ ner Mis _ se _

that, mei _ _ ner Mis _ _ se_that, mei_ner Mis_se_that, bei der Welt

ist gar kein Rath, und __ im Her_zen stehn die Schmerzen mei_ner Mis _ se _ that, weil der Knecht

nei _ _ net, der doch auf ein'n ern _ sten Blick bit _ ter _ li _ _ chen

nei _ _ net, der doch auf ein'n ern _ sten Blick bit _ ter _ li _ _ chen

nei _ _ net, der doch auf ein'n ern _ sten Blick bit _ ter _ li _ _ chen

nei _ _ net, der doch auf ein'n ern _ sten Blick bit _ ter _ li _ _ chen

wei _ _ _ net: Je _ su, bli _ _ cke mich auch an, wenn ich nicht will

wei _ _ _ net: Je _ su, bli _ _ cke mich auch an, wenn ich nicht will

wei _ _ _ net: Je _ su, bli _ _ cke mich auch an, wenn ich nicht will

wei _ _ _ net: Je _ su, bli _ _ cke mich auch an, wenn ich nicht will

bü _ _ _ ssen; wenn ich Bö _ ses hab' ge _ than, rüh _ re mein Ge _ wis _ _ sen.

bü _ _ _ ssen; wenn ich Bö _ ses hab' ge _ than, rüh _ re mein Ge _ wis _ _ sen.

bü _ _ _ ssen; wenn ich Bö _ ses hab' ge _ than, rüh _ re mein Ge _ wis _ _ sen.

bü _ _ _ ssen; wenn ich Bö _ ses hab' ge _ than, rüh _ re mein Ge _ wis _ _ sen.

Fine della prima parte.

SECOND PART

43

CHORAL.

RECITATIVO.

45

48

52

CHORAL.

Soprano. Flauto traverso I. II. Oboe I. Violino I. col Soprano.

Alto. Oboe II. Violino II. coll' Alto.

Tenore. Viola col Tenore.

Basso.

Organo e Continuo.

Stromenti

V.1. Ach, gro_sser Kö_nig, gross zu al_len Zei___ten, wie

V.1. Ach, gro_sser Kö_nig, gross zu al_len Zei___ten, wie

V.2. Ich kann's mit mei_nen Sin_nen nicht er_rei___chen, wo_

V.2. Ich kann's mit mei_nen Sin_nen nicht er_rei___chen, wo_

kann ich g'nug_sam die_se Treu' aus_brei___ten? Kein's Men_schen Her_ze

kann ich g'nug_sam die_se Treu' aus_brei___ten? Kein's Men_schen Her_ze

mit doch dein Er_bar_men zu ver_glei___chen. Wie kann ich dir denn

mit doch dein Er_bar_men zu ver_glei___chen. Wie kann ich dir denn

mag in_dess aus_den___ken, was dir zu schen___ken.

mag in_dess aus__den___ken, was dir zu schen__ken.

dei_ne Lie_bes_tha___ten im Werk er_stat___ten?

dei_ne Lie_bes_tha__ten im Werk er_stat___ten?

53

CORO.

Flauto traverso I. II.
Oboe I. Violino I.

Soprano.
Oboe II. col Soprano.

Nicht diesen, diesen nicht, nicht diesen, sondern Bar _ ra _ bam, nicht diesen, sondern

Alto.
Violino II. coll' Alto.

Nicht diesen, diesen nicht, nicht diesen, sondern Bar _ ra _ bam, nicht diesen, sondern

Tenore.
Viola col Tenore.

Nicht diesen, diesen nicht, nicht diesen, sondern Bar _ ra _ bam, nicht diesen, sondern

Basso.

Nicht diesen, diesen nicht, nicht die _ sen, sondern Bar _ rabam, nicht diesen, sondern

Organo e Continuo.

Bar _ rabam, Bar _ rabam!

Bar _ rabam, Bar _ rabam!

Bar _ rabam, Bar _ rabam!

RECITATIVO.
Evangelist.

Barrabas a _ ber war ein Mörder. Da nahm Pi _ la _ tus Jesum und gei _ _ _ _ _

Bar _ rabam, Bar _ rabam!

_ _ sselte ihn.

Himmelsschlüsselblu_me blüht; du kannst viel süsse Frucht von sei_ner Wermuth brechen, drum

sieh' ohn' Unterlass auf Ihn, auf Ihn, drum sieh' ohn' Un_terlass auf Ihn, ohn' Un_

__terlass, drum sieh' ohn' Un_terlass auf Ihn.

ARIA.

Viola d'amore I.

Viola d'amore II.

Tenore.

Organo e Continuo.

sein blut_gefärbter Rücken in allen Stücken, in allen Stücken dem Himmel glei _ _ _ _ che, dem Himmel gleiche

geht!

Da _ ran,   nachdem die Wasserwo _ _ _ _ _ gen von unsrer Sündfluth sich ver _ zo _

gen, der aller_schönste Re_gen_bo _ _ _ _ _ _ _

_ _gen als Got_tes Gna_den_zei_ _chen steht,_____als Got_tes Gna_ _ _den_zei_chen

RECITATIVO.
Evangelist.

Evangelist. Und die Kriegsknech _ te floch _ ten ei _ ne Kro _ ne von Dor _ nen, und

Organo e Continuo.

setz_ten sie auf sein Haupt, und leg_ten ihm ein Pur_pur_kleid an, und spra_chen:

RECITATIVO.

74

Soprano.
Flauto traverso I.II.
Oboe I.II. Violino I.
col Soprano.

Alto.
Violino II. coll'Alto.

Tenore.
Viola col Tenore.

Basso.

Organo e Continuo.

CHORAL.

Durch dein Ge_fäng_niss, Got_tes Sohn, ist uns die Frei_heit kom__men,
Dein Ker_ker ist der Gna_den_thron, die Frei_statt al__ler From__men;

denn gingst du nicht die Knecht_schaft ein, müsst' un_sre Knechtschaft e__wig sein.

RECITATIVO.
Evangelist.

Evangelist.

Die Ju_den a_ber schrie_en und

Organo e Continuo.

RECITATIVO.

_zige, kreu _ _ _ _ zige, kreu _ _ zige, kreu _ _ _ _ zige ihn!

ihn, kreu _ _ zige, kreu _ _ zige ihn, kreu _ _ _ _ zige,kreuzige ihn!

ihn, kreu _ _ _ _ _ zige ihn, kreu _ _ _ zige,kreuzige ihn!

ihn, kreu _ _ _ _ zige ihn, kreuzige,kreu _ _ _ _ _ zige ihn!

RECITATIVO.

Evangelist. Pilatus. Evangelist.

Evangelist.
Pilatus.

Spricht Pi_latus zu | ihnen: Soll ich euren Kö_nig | kreuzigen? Die Hohen_priester antworteten:

Organo e
Continuo.

CORO.

Flauto traverso I. II.

Oboe I. Violino I.

Oboe d'amore. Violino II.

Viola.

Soprano.

Wir, wir, wir ha _ ben kei _ nen Kö _ nig, wir

Alto.

Wir, wir, wir ha _ ben kei _ nen Kö _ nig, wir

Tenore.

Wir, wir, wir ha _ ben kei _ nen Kö _ nig, wir

Basso.

Wir, wir, wir ha _ ben kei _ nen Kö _ nig, wir

Organo e Continuo.

Wohin? wohin? wo hin? wohin? wohin? wohin?

Wohin? wohin? wo hin? wohin? wohin? wohin?

Wohin? wohin? wo hin? wohin? wohin? wohin?

eilt, _____ eilt,

wohin? wohin? wohin?

wohin? wohin? wohin?

wohin? wohin? wohin?

eilt, eilt nach Gol _ gatha! eilt _____

wohin? wohin? wohin? wohin? wohin? wohin? wohin? wohin?

wohin? wohin? wohin? wohin? wohin? wohin? wohin? wohin?

wohin? wohin? wohin? wohin? wohin? wohin? wohin? wohin?

flieht, flieht, flieht zum

wohin?

wohin?

wohin?

Kreu_zes Hü _ _ _ gel, flieht zum Kreuzes Hügel, eu _ _ re Wohl

Dal Segno.

94

CORO.

CHORAL.

die ge_kränkten Seelen, o Trost, o Trost! es ist voll_bracht, o Trost für die gekränkten See_

len, die Trauer_nacht,

die Trauer_nacht _____ lässt mich die letzte Stun_de, die letz_te Stun_de zäh_len,

die Trauer_nacht lässt mich die letzte Stun_de zählen. Der

Macht, der Held aus Ju_da siegt mit Macht, und schliesst den Kampf,

Adagio.

und schliesst den Kampf. Es ist vollbracht!

RECITATIVO.

Evangelist.

Evangelist.

Es ist vollbracht!

Organo e
Continuo.

Und neigte das Haupt und verschied.

du das Haupt____ und sprichst stillschweigend: Ja, stillschweigend, still_schweigend: Ja! doch neigest du das

Haupt und sprichst still _ schwei _ gend: Ja! *forte*

RECITATIVO. (Ev. St. Matthaei, Cap. 27, V. 51-52.)

Evangelist.

Und sie_he da, der Vor_hang im Tem_pel zer_riss in zwei Stück von

Evangelist.

Organo e Continuo.

o_ben an bis un_ten aus. Und die Er_de er_be_be_te, und die Fel_sen zer_

ris_sen, und die Grä_ber thä_ten sich auf, und stunden auf vie_le Lei_ber der Hei _ li_gen!

ARIOSO.

Flauto traverso I.

Flauto traverso II.

Oboe da caccia I.

Oboe da caccia II.

Violino I.

Violino II.

Viola.

Tenore.

Organo e Continuo.

Mein Herz! in dem die ganze Welt bei Je_su Leiden gleichfalls lei _ det, die

Sonne sich in Trau _ er klei_det, der Vorhang reisst, der Fels zerfällt, die Erde bebt, die Gräber

Adagio.

spal _ ten, weil sie den Schöpfer sehn er _ kal _ ten: was willt du dei _ nes Or _ tes thun?

ARIA.

Flauto traverso I.II.

Oboe da caccia I.II.

Soprano.

Organo e Continuo.

zer _ _ flie _ _ sse, mein Her _ _ ze, in Flu _ _ then der Zäh _ _ _ _

forte

_ _ _ ren dem Höchsten zu Eh _ _ _ _ _ ren.

piano

Er _

zäh _ _ le der Welt und dem Him _ mel die Noth, er _ zäh _ _ le der Welt und dem

118

RECITATIVO.

Evangelist.

Evangelist.

Die Ju_den a_ber, die_weil es der Rüsttag war, dass nicht die Leichna_me am Kreu_ze

Organo e Continuo.

blie_ben den Sab_bath ü_ber, (denn des _ sel_bigen Sabbath_tags war sehr gross,) ba_ten sie Pi_la_tum, dass

ih_re Bei_ne ge_brochen, und sie ab_ge_nommen wür_den. Da ka_men die Kriegsknechte und

CHORAL.

Soprano. Flauto traverso I.II. Oboe I.II. Violino I. col Soprano.

Alto. Violino II. coll'Alto.

Tenore. Viola col Tenore.

Basso.

Organo e Continuo.

O hilf, Chri_ste, Got_tes Sohn, durch dein bit_tres Lei_den, dass wir, dir stets un_ter_than, all' Un_tu_gend mei_den; dei_nen Tod und sein' Ur_sach' fruchtbar_lich be_den_ken, da_für, wiewohl arm und schwach, dir Dank_o_pfer schen_ken.

RECITATIVO.
Evangelist.

Evangelist.

Organo e
Continuo.

Dar_nach bat Pi_la_tum Joseph von A_rima_thi_a, der ein Jünger Je_su war, (doch

heimlich aus Furcht vor den Ju_den,) dass er möchte ab_nehmen den Leichnam Je_su. Und Pi_la_tus er_lau_bete

es. De_rowegen kam er und nahm den Leichnam Je_su her_ab. Es kam a_ber auch Ni_co_

de_mus, der vor_mals in der Nacht zu Je_su kommen war, und brachte Myrrhen und A_loen un_ter ein_

an_der, bei hundert Pfun_den. Da nahmen sie den Leichnam Je_su, und bun_den ihn in leinen Tücher mit Spe_ce_

rei_en, wie die Juden pfle_gen zu be_gra_ben. Es war a_ber an der Stät_te, da er ge_

kreu_ziget ward, ein Gar_ten, und im Gar_ten ein neu Grab, in welches Niemand je ge_legen war. Da_

selbst hin leg_ten sie Je_sum, um des Rüsttags wil_len der Ju_den, dieweil das Grab na_he war.

CORO.

125

senza Flauti ed Oboi.

mich zur Ruh'.

mich zur Ruh'.

mich zur Ruh'.

mich zur Ruh'.

Das Grab, so euch ___ be_stim ___ ___

Das Grab, so euch, so euch be_

Das Grab, so euch be_stim ___ ___

Das Grab, so euch be_

Flauti ed Oboi col Violino I.

128

senza Flauti.

bringt auch mich, auch mich ___ zur Ruh', ruht wohl, ruht wohl, ihr hei_li_gen Ge_

wohl, und bringt ___ auch mich zur Ruh', ruht' wohl, ruht wohl, ihr hei_li_gen Ge_

wohl, und bringt auch mich zur Ruh', ruht wohl, ruht wohl, ihr hei_li_gen Ge_

wohl, und bringt auch mich zur Ruh', ruht wohl, ruht wohl, ihr hei_li_gen Ge_

bei_ _ne, die ich nun wei_ _ter nicht be_wei_ne, ruht wohl, ___ ruht

bei_ _ne, die ich nun wei_ _ter nicht be_wei_ne, ruht wohl, ___ ruht

bei_ _ne, die ich nun wei_ _ter nicht be_wei_ne, ruht wohl, ___ ruht

bei_ _ne, die ___ ich nun wei_ _ter nicht be_wei_ _ne, ruht wohl, ___

Flauti col Violino I.

wohl, — und bringt auch mich, und bringt auch mich zur Ruh', — und bringt auch mich zur

wohl, — und bringt auch mich zur Ruh', zur Ruh', und bringt auch mich zur

wohl, — und bringt auch mich zur Ruh', und bringt auch mich zur

— ruht wohl, und bringt auch mich zur Ruh', und bringt auch mich zur

senza Flauti ed Oboi.

Ruh'. Das Grab, so euch — be_stim _ _ _ met ist, und fer_ner kei _ _ ne Noth

Ruh'. Das Grab, so euch — be_stim _ _ _ met ist, und fer_ner kei _ _ ne Noth

Ruh'. Das Grab, so euch be _ stim _ met ist, und fer _ _ _ ner kei _ _ ne

Ruh'.

Flauti
ed Oboi.

__ um _ schliesst, macht mir den Himmel auf, und schliesst __ die Höl _ le zu. Ruht

__ um _ schliesst, macht mir den Himmel auf, und schliesst die Höl _ _ le zu. Ruht

Noth um _ _ schliesst, macht mir den Him _ mel auf, und schliesst die Höl _ le zu. Ruht

Ruht

Ruht

Dal Segno. 𝄋

CHORAL.

Soprano.
Flauto traverso I.
Oboe I. Violino I.
col Soprano.

Alto.
Flauto traverso II.
Oboe II. Violino II.
coll'Alto.

Tenore.
Viola col Tenore.

Basso.

Organo e Continuo.

Ach Herr, lass dein lieb' En _ ge _ lein am letz _ ten End' die
Den Leib in sein'm Schlaf _ käm _ mer _ lein gar sanft, ohn ein' _ _ ge

SUPPLEMENT

A. ARIE und CHORAL.

In the original version of the *St. John Passion*, this piece occurred, following the chorale on page 31.

Je _ _ _ _ _ su, dei _ _ ne Pas _ si _ _ on

ton, fallt in meinen Trau_er_ton, in mei_nen Trau_er_ton, se_het mei _ ne Qual und

ist mir lau _ ter

Angst, _____ meine Qual und Angst, was ich, Je_su, mit dir lei _ _ _ _ _

Freu _ _ de,

_ _ _de! Ja, ich zäh_le dei_ne Schmer _ _ _ _ zen, dei _ ne Schmer _ _ _

Werden auf den Kreuzes _ we _ _ _ _ _ _

Mei _ _ ne Seel' auf Ro _ sen geht,

_ _ gen dei _ ne Dor _ nen aus _ ge _ sä't, werden auf den Kreuzes _ wegen dei _ ne Dor _ nen ausge _ _

sä't, weil ich in Zu _ frie _ den _ heit mich in dei _ ne Wun _ den

wenn ich dran ge _

sen _ ke, mich in dei _ ne Wunden

Stätt'

wenn ein stürmend Wetter weht, diesen Ort, da _ hin ich mich täg _ _ _ lich

durch den Glau _ ben len _ _ _ _ _ _ _ ke, durch den Glau _ _ _ ben

mir des _ _ we _ gen schen _ _ _ ke!

len _ _ _ _ _ _ _ _ _ _ _ _ ke, diesen

B. ARIE.

Present in the original version of the *St. John Passion*, this piece was later replaced
by the tenor aria "Ach, mein sinn," page 34.

(Allegro.)

Zerschmettert mich, zerschmettert mich,ihr Fel_sen und ihr Hü _ gel, ihr

stren_ger Richter wie _ _ _ der; ach! fallt vor ihm, ach! fallt vor ihm in

bit _ _ tern Thrä _ nen

forte

forte

forte

nie _ _ der.

Ja,

Da Capo.

C. ARIE.

Present in the original version of the *St. John Passion*, this piece was later replaced
by the bass arioso "Betrachte, meine Seel'," page 55, and the tenor aria on page 57.

plag _ te Seelen, ach, win _ det euch nicht so, ge _ plag _ te Seelen, bei eu _ rer Kreu _ _ _ zes _ Angst und Qual, ach,

win _ det euch nicht so, ge _ plag _ te See _ len, bei eu _ rer Kreuzes _ Angst und Qual, bei eu _ rer Kreuzes _

Angst und Qual.

Könnt

ihr die un_er_mess'ne Zahl der har_ten Gei_ssel_schlä_ge zählen: so zäh_let auch die

Menge eu_rer Sün_den,ihr wer_det die_se grö_sser fin_den.

Könnt ihr die un_ _er_mess'ne Zahl der

har_ten Gei_ssel_schlä_ge zäh_len: so zäh_let auch die Menge eu_rer Sün_den,

ihr wer_det die_se grö_ _ _ _ _ _ _ _ _ _ _ _

_sser, grö_sser fin _den, ihr wer_det die _ _ _se grö_sser fin_den; so zäh_let auch die Menge

eu_rer Sün_den, ihr wer_det die_se grö_ _ _sser fin _ _ _ _den, ihr werdet die_se

grö _ _ _ _sser_ fin_den.

Da Capo.